The Good Library Manual

With a Charter for Public Libraries

Tim Coates

BERKSHIRE
PUBLISHING GROUP

Great Barrington, Massachusetts, U.S.A.

Published by:
Berkshire Publishing Group LLC
122 Castle Street
Great Barrington, Massachusetts 01230-1506 U.S.A.
www.berkshirepublishing.com

Copy Editor: Kathy Brock
Designer: Anna Myers
Illustrations by Anna Myers

Library of Congress Cataloging-in-Publication Data

Coates, Tim.
 The good library manual / by Tim Coates.
    p. cm.
  ISBN 978-1-933782-88-1 (pbk.)
 1. Public libraries—Administration. 2. Public libraries—Aims and objectives. 3. Libraries and community.
 4. Public libraries—Great Britain—Administration. 5. Public libraries—Aims and objectives—Great Britain.
 6. Libraries and community—Great Britain. I. Title.
 Z678.C65 2010
 025.1'974—dc22
                                                 2010030963
 Z678.C65 2010
 025.1'974—dc22

                                                 2010030963

Praise for *The Good Library Manual:*

"Rethink your library! Let bookstore merchandising and marketing guru Tim Coates show you the way. *The Good Library Manual* is just the ticket to ensuring that your library is, indeed, the center of your community and the most prized destination in town."

—**Sally Gardner Reed**, *Executive Director, Association of Library Trustees, Advocates, Friends and Foundations, U.S.A.*

"Tim Coates brings an informed eye to the world of public libraries. Always challenging and provocative, Tim demands to be read."

—**Alan Gibbons**, *author of* Shadow of the Minotaur *and other children's books, U.K.*

"Tim Coates knows more about libraries and how to make them better than any number of management consultants or quangos."

—**Richard Charkin**, *Executive Director, Bloomsbury Publishing, U.K./U.S.A.*

"Tim Coates shows local libraries that have been transformed, and that in turn transformed the way local people view and use their libraries."

—**Mavis Cheek**, *author of* Pause Between Acts *and other novels, U.K.*

"Tim Coates' passion, imagination, and determination are an inspiration for all of us."

—**Hugh Andrew**, *Birlinn Publishers, Edinburgh, U.K.*

"This is a beautiful book, the advice is practical and upbeat, and it's delivered in a delightful style. It's for anyone who wants to see public libraries thrive."

—**Kathleen Zaenger**, *Director, Howell Carnegie District Library, Michigan, U.S.A. (one of the libraries featured in* Heart of the Community: The Libraries We Love, *Berkshire Publishing Group, 2007)*

"Libraries are our future—to close them would be a terrible, terrible mistake—it would be stealing from the future to pay for today, which is what got us into the mess we're in now."

—**Neil Gaiman**, *author of* American Gods *and other award-winning fantasy and science fiction books, in his acceptance speech for the Carnegie Medal in Literature, U.K.*

Berkshire Publishing has hosted the **Good Library Blog** (www.goodlibraryguide.com/blog) since 2006. The blog uses the imaginary Carnegie Library by the dockside at Bloggington on Sea as a model for how libraries should be run. A series of entries on the blog describe the methods and practices of its librarians.

Perkins, a small black cat with golden eyes (illustrated on the book's cover and at left), is the ruler of the Good Library Blog. She took control after a newspaper printed a citizen's comment, "My cat could run the public library service better than those in charge." Perkins is not her real name. It is a "nom-de-blogue" to cover her true identity. She has a role in most of the stories about the library at Bloggington on Sea. She sleeps above the reference department's radiator in the space left by missing volumes of an extensive work of local history.

Perkins became notorious when she gave a new name to the Chartered Institute of Library and Information Professionals, the United Kingdom's professional body of librarians generally known by the acronym CILIP; Perkins changed the group's name to SYRUP because of their reluctance to move forward and their slow progress. For that, she has been awarded both praise and damnation.

The Good Library Blog
www.goodlibraryguide.com/blog

Contents

> For Philip Pettifor

Acknowledgments

I would like to thank the many people who have supported my efforts in the field of public libraries. They have contributed in many ways and helped to shape this book. My thanks go to the councillors, officers, and residents of the London Borough of Hillingdon; the trustees of the charities Libri, Laser, and the Robert Gavron Charitable Trust; the officers of English councils in Westminster, Portsmouth, Tower Hamlets, Cumbria, Ealing, Richmond, Hampshire, Oxfordshire, and others; the committee and members of Libraries for Life for Londoners; those who have commented on the Good Library Guide Blog; the staff and journalists of the Bookseller and many U.K. newspapers, who have covered the developments with great interest; Roy Clare, the Museums, Libraries and Archives Council, the Department of Culture, Media and Sport, the Chartered Institute of Library and Information Professionals, the Advisory Council on Libraries, the Society of Chief Librarians, the Reading Agency, the Improvement and Development Agency, and the Audit Commission; several members of Parliament and their researchers; Shirley Burnham and the people of Old Town Swindon and the Wirral; the management and staff at Talis and other library management systems suppliers; the management and staff of many library book suppliers; Rupert Wheeler and Mackenzie Wheeler Architects and Designers; graphic designers David Carroll and Rob Andrew; the Library Campaign and the Campaign for the Book; Christopher Hawtree, John Whelan, Hugh Andrew, Richard Charkin, Susan Hill, Margaret Yorke, Desmond Clarke, Graham Hinton, Nik Pettifor, Alan Gibbons, Jonathan Gibbs, and many publishers, booksellers, and members of the Society of Authors; the people of Bloggington on Sea and readers everywhere; my family and Perkins the cat; and Karen Christensen (CEO), Trevor Young (IT), Rachel Christensen (editorial assistant), and all at Berkshire Publishing Group.

Tim Coates
London

Why Berkshire Publishing Loves Libraries

Tanzhe Temple in western Beijing is one of China's best-known temples. I visited there in June 2010 and was photographed in front of one of its treasures—a carved fish that was, according to folklore, a gift from the Daoist ruler of heaven.

Libraries have a special place in people's hearts, as quotations throughout this book testify. Libraries have a special role in society, too. They offer us a unique kind of public space focused on ideas and information, a space that connects us with a wider world as well as with people and activities in our own communities. Libraries ought to be key focal points in the global communications network, vital points of contact linking individuals and communities, both in person and online, to the larger world that is so much with us today. Many libraries (in the tiniest of towns and the largest of cities) have had a hard time in recent years because of tight funding, modern systems, and new demands—but many have recreated themselves, too, and become once again the heart of their communities.

Some readers of *The Good Library Manual* may never have seen the inside of a library book with the date stamping system pictured opposite. We include this photo not because we think libraries should go back to date stamping by hand, but because of a special kind of continuity it reveals. And there's a global story behind the image. I was in Beijing in June 2010, and I remembered that one of my favorite books, *Peking Picnic* by Ann Bridge, was set largely at Tanzhe Temple, just outside the city. So one afternoon I made the trip, and the photo above was taken in front of a carved stone fish supposedly given to the temple by the Jade Emperor, the legendary Daoist ruler of heaven.

When I got home, I decided to reread *Peking Picnic* and see just how much the city and the temple had changed. I couldn't find my copy, so I took the easy way out. I used the online interlibrary loan, and within a few days a copy was waiting for me at Mason Library (shown on page 10). It had come from the Forbes Library in Northampton, Massachusetts, and had, as you can see, been checked out by many other people since 1937. I had been focused on how much China has changed during the decades since the

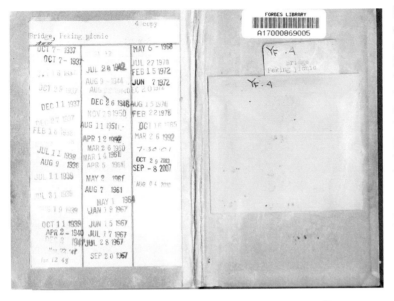

book was written, but the columns of dates (shown in the photograph above right) made me think about how much western Massachusetts, too, has changed. The date stamps, which end with my own due date of Aug 04 2010, made me realize that I am part of a community of people interested in China, tied to this place but also thinking about the wider world.

Peking Picnic is the story of a group of foreigners in China during the 1930s warlord period. The main character, the intellectual wife of an English diplomat, reflects on how we humans connect to particular places and yet somehow manage, practically and imaginatively, to live global lives, adjust to new vistas, and learn to see the world from other

The antiquated due-date ink stamps in this 1937 copy of *Peking Picnic* illustrate a perennial interest in stories from other parts of the globe.

perspectives. These things are fundamental to what Berkshire Publishing tries to do, and also, in a broader sense, to what libraries are. Some libraries have struggled over technology in the effort to stay relevant recently, but we hope *The Good Library Manual* will enable us to focus on what libraries offer to individuals of all ages, to civic well-being, and to society at large through their role as the "commons" for our global village.

This book aims to help any library—U.S. or U.K., large or small, urban or rural—make the most of its assets. Those of us involved in its creation—author Tim Coates, along with the many people who've worked with him in the United Kingdom and also the team at Berkshire Publishing, who have drawn on the wealth of material in the previously published *Heart of the Community: The Libraries We Love*—are inspired by our personal experiences with libraries. I am delighted to be able to publish *The Good Library Manual* and look forward to working with Tim Coates and all the hundreds of librarians and community leaders on both sides of the Atlantic and in other parts of the world who share our conviction that libraries make the world a better place.

Karen Christensen
Great Barrington, Massachusetts

Introduction

This library has a cluttered, jumbled look, which certainly won't attract the people we are trying convince to make libraries part of their lives again. Thirty years ago, bookshops used to think this look was acceptable, but they can't afford to think that way today, and neither can libraries.

In England, instead of libraries being valued as libraries, it became necessary for them to demonstrate that they were contributing to other government agendas. Libraries, it was said, had to play a role in combating climate change and obesity, or even in promoting the Olympic Games. All these different goals just confused the people who were actually running the library, and it confused the public, too.

Even before the drastic public spending cuts that began in 2010, the public library service in England was in trouble. While it had been well funded by the state for many years, successive governments had called upon libraries to offer such a variety of social services that their whole sense of purpose had been lost. The once famous and treasured book collections had been allowed to dwindle to the point of uselessness, if not extinction. Book lending—the libraries' main function—had halved. Visitor numbers had fallen.

All those attempts to attract a wider audience through "diversification" had diminished the reputation of the public library service. Two generations of citizens (that is, almost everyone except the smallest children and the oldest adults) had come to wonder if there is really a reason for libraries to exist. In turn, this loss of relevance to many people led to a loss of support and funding from the local government officials, councils, and councillors who used to provide so generously.

But this situation can be changed, with the combined efforts of community leaders, librarians, educators, authors, and readers of all ages and interests. In England, we are in the early stages of an effort to restore our public libraries. I was a bookseller for many years and became involved when I innocently stepped in to offer solutions drawn from my experience creating successful bookstores. I believed that there were fairly straightforward solutions to the problems faced by libraries, solutions which can be used anyplace, in any country, by anyone who wants to make their library a popular and valued place. I believed then, and still believe today, that the library service can be restored and made sustainable through proper planning and management. *The Good Library Manual* contains examples of my work in England as well as photographs of successful and beautiful libraries in the United States.

How to Run a Library

This book contains two kinds of practical advice to help librarians and Friends of Libraries groups properly operate libraries: advice for everyday library operations and guidelines for a library makeover. In everyday operations, you'll want to consider the physical aspects of your library, including the layout of the entryway, displays, and study areas. During a library makeover, you'll want to address areas such as the stock, the attractiveness and suitability of the building, and the operating hours.

It is hard and takes practice, but you have to see your library as strangers see it and make it so they find it attractive and inviting. Some people do this naturally, but some don't, just as some people dress in a stylish way, and some don't. But in a public library, we are on public show—we must look smart. Some people don't care what we look like, but we have to dress for those who do care. You'll want to look at four aspects of your library's layout: the exterior, inside the front door, the displays, and the study area.

Exterior

Stand 10 meters away from the library, or across the street or even up the road a bit. Take a long, critical look. Imagine that you are a newcomer to town, visiting the library for the first time. The following standards should help you evaluate your library's exterior:

- The front windows must be clean, bright, and arresting.
- The window displays should entice someone outside to come and see what is inside. Whether books or a clear view of the library interior, it must be a stage set—brilliant, bright, and inviting.
- The steps, pavement, and paintwork must be in good condition and clean.
- Signs must be professional, clear, clean, and legible.

Many library buildings, old and new, are attractive and well designed. Make sure that your library retains these qualities. Don't spoil them with bad signage or other changes which detract from the original features. Don't stick things to the windows—inside or out! If your library has used designers to improve your graphics or your presentation, follow their rule book. Don't ignore their work and don't destroy what they have thought about.

What you see from a distance is the best advertisement for the library. It must be attractive and interesting.

Whether historic or contemporary, a library's exterior should be attentively maintained to welcome visitors.

Historic elegance meets modern convenience in this library's new addition.

Opposite: We don't need advertising boards for libraries if we use the buildings as the attraction.

This shuttered library in south London is on Death Row.

Most librarians came to the profession because they care about books and love to read. Working in a library that is meeting the needs of its patrons is a satisfying profession.

Opposite: A library should be like a traditional English pub in which the landlord (the librarian) becomes part of the community and the place is everybody's "local." Amenities like this library's coffee bar can foster this sense of connection.

Modern or traditional, large or small, the best libraries are a warm and welcoming place for the communities they serve.

From time to time, pick a few favourite shops, restaurants, or pubs, and stand outside them. Ask yourself two questions:

- Do the individuals who own and run this establishment look like interesting people who will be nonintrusive, friendly, and welcoming, or do they look like difficult people who will require you to behave in a way that makes you uncomfortable?
- Do they have something inside that is worth exploring, browsing through, or just enjoying, or might their wares be dowdy and disappointing?

Against these two measures, give both your favourite places and your library a score—it may help identify what you can improve. Ask others who don't work in the library to do the same, and then see what they tell you. Good presentation isn't always about spending money; it is about seeing things as others see them.

Inside the Front Door

Now enter your library and find out whether the staff follows these important standards:

- Vacuum the carpet and the floors every day.
- Make sure all the lights are working every day—no flashing fluorescents, no dirty bulbs or deflectors.
- Use notice boards and keep them current, attractive, and interesting. Liberally use display materials from the community, but present them tidily and neatly. People are proud of their posters.

Libraries often exhibit bad habits in their appearance and lack of tidiness. But their walls essentially serve as notice boards of local information—more useful than anything online. Patrons should feel welcome to offer suggestions and provide materials for the library to disseminate.

The reception desk gives patrons their first impression of your library. Patrons should see, and feel, that the library is there for them. You sometimes see clutter at the reception desk, but there is no need for it. It sends out the message that "this place is run for the convenience of those who have to work here." That's wrong.

Healthy plants create a welcoming environment and improve the air quality, too.

- Don't put reusable adhesive putty or cellophane tape on walls, wooden furniture, or counters.
- Keep the service counters tidy and uncluttered. Don't use the shelves underneath the counters for storage. Keep them clean and neat.
- Make sure all the windows, blinds, and shutters are clean.
- Make sure all the interior signs are clear, clean, and well lit. Check whether any legislation has special requirements for people with disabilities. For example, in the United Kingdom, the Disability Discrimination Act (DDA) includes requirements about lettering which are intended to make everything easy to see and read.
- Any flowers or plants should be alive, thriving, and looked after.
- Staff should be smartly groomed.
- Check that display posters are straight and properly hung. If possible, make sure the books they advertise are visible nearby.

Compare your library with the lobby of a really smart hotel. Look good!

Here are lively displays for books about animals and for the Young People's Library. This makes it easy for visitors to find something new.

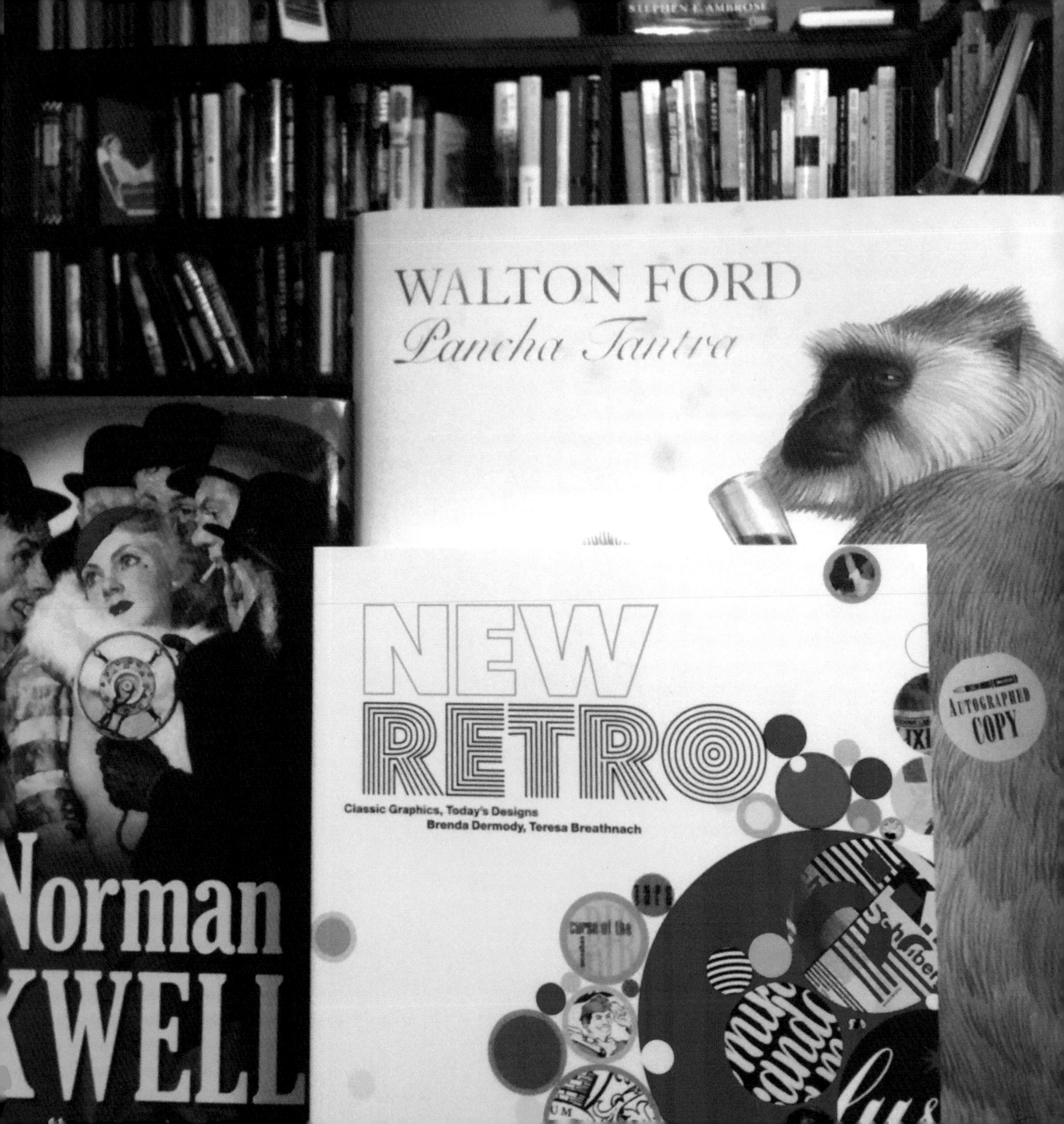

WALTON FORD
Pancha Tantra

NEW RETRO

Classic Graphics, Today's Designs
Brenda Dermody, Teresa Breathnach

Norman
KWELL

AUTOGRAPHED
COPY

Displays

Examine your library's displays. Your library staff should be following these guidelines:

A retailer checks every display every day to make sure that the signs are clear and the shelves are full and dusted. Patrons should never be confused by incorrect classification labels.

Opposite: Attractive book displays are fascinating, and book-jacket design is a great art. Make the displays full and exciting.

- Dust the shelves on a regular rota so that the library is completely cleaned each week. Make sure every shelf display is tidy and presented in a professional manner—no books fallen over, no empty shelves because the classification needs moving.
- Put books back in the correct place every day. Clear the returns and place the new stock so that there is no backlog.
- Weed the stock every day so that as much stock is leaving as is arriving. This will allow you to keep the shelves full all the time and not have gaps in the display.
- Adjust the classification signs constantly so that they deliver their promise. A sign that says GARDENING BOOKS should represent as comprehensive a collection of topics about gardening as library space permits.

Consider what you have in the smallest chosen library. A company of the wisest and wittiest men that could be picked out of all civil countries, in a thousand years, have set in best order the results of their learning and wisdom. The men themselves were hid and inaccessible, solitary, impatient of interruption, fenced by etiquette; but the thought which they did not uncover to their bosom friend is here written out in transparent words to us, the strangers of another age.

—RALPH WALDO EMERSON

This is the study area in a small English village library. Before its makeover, it was grim and dim, but natural light and an attractive, simple interior design have transformed the building into a lovely and popular library.

- Use smartly prepared shelf-edge labels to subdivide a category or to highlight particular authors or subjects.
- Don't use signs to indicate oversize books unless absolutely necessary; adjust the shelves if you can.
- Use all the shelves to make displays which attractively mix books with the spine facing out and the front cover facing out. Pull the face-out books to the front of the shelf with display blocks. Use the top and bottom shelves. The important thing is to have as wide a selection as possible of the best books on the topics within a category.

Don't sit behind the front desk waiting for readers. Move around the library, just as a retailer does. It is always possible to make displays more attractive.

I received the fundamentals of my education in school, but that was not enough. My real education, the superstructure, the details, the true architecture, I got out of the public library. For an impoverished child whose family could not afford to buy books, the library was the open door to wonder and achievement, and I can never be sufficiently grateful that I had the wit to charge through that door and make the most of it. Now, when I read constantly about the way in which library funds are being cut and cut, I can only think that the door is closing and that American society has found one more way to destroy itself.

—ISAAC ASIMOV

Opposite: The reading room at the Mason Library, Great Barrington, Massachusetts, which was described as "the most exquisitely complete piece of architectural design which has appeared in a long time" by *Architecture* magazine in 1913.

Study Areas

Areas for private reading, study, or computer use are an important part of the library's function. Review your library's study areas to ensure that they meet these specifications:

- Make sure that that the desks, surfaces, and chairs are cleaned every day.
- Make sure that computer screens and keyboards are also clean.
- If you have comfortable armchairs and sofas, keep them tidy and make sure they give the readers privacy. Don't gather them around one table as if they were for a group in conversation; put them in quiet corners.

Respect people's privacy, dignity, work, and study. Make sure that other readers do the same.

Study areas and public computers are the unique selling point of a public library. Think of creating the atmosphere of a comfortable, spacious lobby at a historic hotel.

Opposite: For many people, the only place they can get a peaceful, quiet, dignified place to read quietly or concentrate on their work is in the public library. Make it an appealing place to read and study, not somewhere with all the ambiance of a police station or hospital waiting room.

People generally talk about individual libraries being part of the community, but reading and studying are very private activities. To be allowed to read what you choose, quietly and on your own, is one of the greatest advances civilization ever made.

Library Makeover

Managing a library service, like managing a retail operation, is half about what the public sees and half about what goes on behind the scenes. People who use, or would use, libraries are most interested in three things: what is available (the stock); whether the building is attractive and suitable; and when the building is open (the hours). The makeover is an opportunity to transform all three. During a makeover, you'll also want to think about the role of the staff, behind-the-scenes activities, and, of course, launch plans for your new library.

Stock, Layout, and Space Allocation

Just like a bookshop, a library's stock is divided into categories. Every library is different, and each should match the particular requirements of its local community. When undertaking a makeover of your library, you should start with a list of the community's needs. Your primary emphasis should be that which makes your community different: if your library is located in a place with a particularly interesting history, put that at the top of your list of priorities for space allocation. You will designate the remaining space to all those topics which interest everyone, but you should emphasise those which characterise your area. The obvious example is the collection for small children, which will be greater in a small local library used as a meeting place for children than in a city centre with a much older population.

The signs you put up make a tremendous difference to the sense of place of the building.

Public libraries date to the ninth-century Middle East, but the modern public library movement began in the 1800s. In some countries with great heritage, the library is the most important national institution. Our role is to cherish and pass on our libraries in a better state than we received them, not to be so clever that we destroy them.

Designers of libraries have concentrated far too much on the exterior architecture. Put a library in the hands of a clever interior designer and you can make it a lovely place to be in.

GHT ALICE WITHOUT PICTURES OR CONVERSATION? AND AC

ONCE THERE WERE FOUR CHILI

SUSAN, EDMUND AND LUCY. T

THAT HAPPENED TO THEM WH

LED WHEN MR. BILBO BAGGINS OF BAG END ANNOUNCED THA

UG. BE CELEBRATING HIS ELEVENTY-FIRST BIRTHDAY WITH

MAGNIFICENCE, THERE WAS MUCH TALK AND EXCITEM

CHILDRENS

Finding out about the interests and demographics of your community can improve your library's collection and help it appeal to many generations.

Library authorities and local government officials have often told people that it is too difficult to renovate old and precious buildings for use as libraries. This is not true. The building on the right is over four hundred years old. And if we think of the number of restaurants and stylish retailers who have turned old buildings into wonderful places to spend time, we realise the problem is only a question of finding an experienced interior designer who knows how to handle these projects.

Libraries should allocate their shelves to different subjects in proportion to the interests of the people who might use them; allocation should not be determined by how much stock there is. Of all the elements needed to make a library successful at lending books, the two most important are allocation and the stock selection itself.

In this way, determine how much space and emphasis you would like to give to different subjects and categories. There are lists which show how reading habits differ and, for example, the proportion of the population who reads fiction or uses cookery books. These lists are available from your book supplier. Your ideal space allocation is a description of your understanding of the reading needs and interests of your local community, not a reflection of how many books you have on different subjects. If the library hasn't got books on fishing, it is of no use to an aspiring fisherman. You may also have too few of some and too many of others; a makeover is an opportunity to correct this imbalance.

You should find a way of asking both your readers and your "lapsed users" for their views about your stock, either in discussion by giving out simple questionnaires, or using one of the online survey sites to contact your readers and get their opinions. Ask some teachers and local booksellers to comment in detail on your stock. They will give you a load of good advice.

If you are a librarian and have a local Friends of Libraries group, you must involve them from the very start of makeover or renovation discussions to hear what they think and feel. In a similar way, research the newspapers and journals appropriate for your local community—particularly any that the library may not have stocked in the past but which may reflect changes in the area.

Now make a list of how much display space you wish to devote to different categories of books. Then do the same for films and music, if your library has space for these items, too.

Entr

This Tiffany window, titled *Instruction*, was donated to the Chatham Public Library, Chatham, New York, in 1908.

Opposite: Paper, pencil, cardboard, ruler, scissors, and public feedback are all that are needed to start planning a library makeover. To make a scale drawing of the library, keep it simple: one centimeter for every meter, for example. Or photocopy the architectural drawings for the building, if available.

Having allocated space to detailed categories, you need to acquire the best stock to make the collections. Obviously you will be limited by your budget, but this work is the most important. It is surprising how few people realise that 90 percent or more of what people read (fiction and nonfiction) is "backlist," which means it was first published over a year ago. Good collections are predominantly backlist. Don't use your makeover money exclusively on "front list" items. The front list adds style and fashion, but the backlist is larger and used more. Look at each section you have identified on your plan and purchase new copies of the leading backlist. Some titles and topics are essential, and you must have them; some are important, but there are alternatives for them. Your library book supplier or a retail wholesaler will happily tell you what those titles are, and, if need be, you will find them in a good bookstore or another library. Personal book-cataloging websites such as LibraryThing, Goodreads and Shelfari can also be very useful in building collection lists. Don't be afraid of snooping round the stock of bookshops with a notepad. They do it to you! (If they ask what you are doing, say you are a schoolteacher.)

Attractive and Suitable Building

There may be a tight limit on the funds available for a refit. But however much is available, you should start by planning the layout of the whole building. Determining how much space you can afford to refurbish expensively can come later, but your rough plan is essential, and its cost is mainly in your time and thought.

As with your stock, find a way to ask local people—users and nonusers—to talk about the library building, especially what they like about it now and what they would like to see changed. Do this by getting them to talk about actual visits they have made to the library or bookshops. Ask these kinds of questions about their past experience: "When did you last go to X's shop?" "What did you buy?" "How did you find it?"

The best way to plan the layout of a library is to make a scale drawing of the building's outline and place pieces of card stock or wood blocks, scaled to match the furniture and display cabinets on it. This helps you think with an open mind about the possible layouts without worrying about how things are now. Every building is different, but you should watch for the following points:

- Make the entrance area as welcoming and attractive as possible. Don't allow your visitors to feel they are being watched or they need permission to come in. Many shops nowadays place the cash registers or ATMs out of sight of the entrance so that people start browsing as soon as they cross the threshold.
- People entering like to have a sense of the scale of the room that they have come into, so make some sight lines clear to the ends of the building.

- Try to place the area for small children well away from the quiet study and reading areas so that children can enjoy themselves, and adults can work without distractions.
- Try to divide the space into rooms that seem like generous sitting rooms. Put tall bookcases around the wall and use them to form alcoves and quiet corners. Break up the space in this way so that it feels comfortable.
- Don't make service counters larger than they absolutely need to be. Don't let them become the central or dominant feature of the library. In fact, the transactions at a library counter are less complex than those at most shop checkouts, so there is no need for them to be large structures.
- Don't use entrance and exit checkout gates, but do use unobtrusive electronic security shields and traffic counters near the main doors. Don't make a feature out of them.
- Use surveillance cameras to watch any places where cash is handled and any other parts of the library that may be of concern.
- Place lending and inquiry counters where staff can have a good view of the library floor. Avoid having more positions than necessary.
- Use some windows to allow natural light to come in. At the same time, it is most important to make the maximum use of the space available. Remember, your library is more useful the more stock it has in it, which might help readers find what they are looking for. So if you cover windows with display fixtures, make sure the space behind them is well lit and accessible to staff.
- Discuss the layout and visit shops, hotels, and other public buildings for ideas.
- Many library staff have the misconception that laws against disability discrimination (such as the United Kingdom's Disability Discrimination Act or the U.S. Americans with Disabilities Act) apply in special ways to libraries, particularly regarding the height of displays. In fact, antidiscrimination law concerns all public entities, including shops, and everyone must adapt and alter premises and layouts accordingly. What you see in other locales, particularly those of larger retailers, will conform to the law.

Having assembled your research and your opinions, you should now seek shop fitters or designers to discuss the next stage (it is normally not necessary to go to an architect). Retailers often work within very tight budgets and timescales for their refit work. They all seek competitive bids from shop fitters, and they normally never allow their premises to be closed to the public while renovation is in progress. Retailers demand that work be done quickly and cleanly to a well-prepared plan with minimum disruption.

The division of space according to its use is one of the most important themes in library renovation. Many libraries put bookcases down the middle of the room, but we would never do that in our own sitting rooms. Like the harmonies of music, interior architecture has certain rhythms to which we respond. We feel comfortable in a reading room which is not too big, where the books are around the walls, and where the furniture is placed in a certain way.

Opposite: You know that coming into a beautiful building—a cathedral or a hall or a fine shop or house—is one of the best feelings that you can get. A library can be like that.

Too many libraries make the counter the centrepiece of the whole design, like a machine-gun position. The librarians are not the most important thing in the room, and people don't want them to be the centre of attraction. Nowadays, stores keep help desks discretely to the side, so that people see what is on offer.

Sadly, libraries lose a lot of books, not only from what retailers euphemistically call "shrinkage" but also because of loans that are never returned. Loss has happened with or without checkout gates. Don't use gates—they are old-fashioned and forbidding.

To read, you need light. Always keep the light fixtures clean and bright, like this comfortable library on the opposite page.

One option to consider seriously, if your budget is tight, is to refit only the first 10 meters inside the library. This normally includes the main window areas and the most important displays. It also includes the parts that get the most wear. A shop fitter should be very happy to accept such a small project and short timetable. If you can do this during the retail peak season (October–January) when fitters are short of work, you may find you get a bargain price. The shop fitter and their own design team will finish off your rough layout plan and make sure it conforms to all legal requirements, and they will use it as a basis for their own planning.

Lighting a library is one of the most important tasks. The display shelves, the study areas, and the windows need to be lit brightly and "locally." Modern bookstores have addressed these problems, and other retailers have learned to make their stores much brighter than they used to be. At the same time, the fittings need to be reasonably inexpensive and long lasting.

You must make sure that everything for your refit is planned, and all issues are settled before anyone lifts a hammer. Somebody has to be in charge of dealings with the builders and fitters, and the lines of responsibility must be clear. The timetable might change because of unforeseen circumstances, but there should be none of those at the outset.

If the shop fitter is to work in phases (that is, in one section of the library while the others remain open), you will need to move stock when the plan requires, normally when the library is not open to the public. Be ready for that and have plenty of people available to help.

A refit is a difficult time, even if everything works to plan, because of the dirt and the discomfit. Be ready. Readers might complain but you mustn't—it is their inconvenience that has to concern you. Put up plenty of notices explaining to the public what is happening and the timetable; apologize for the disruption of services. Make sure you have made clear arrangements for anything that might affect them.

Old bookcases are wonderful things. So are the old collections of books that are stored in the basements of libraries. Bring them out into the open and make them available to readers to explore on a rainy day.

Opening hours should be long and regular—like shop hours.

Libraries are so popular and well understood that there is no need to spend money on advertising your library makeover. Schoolchildren will do a perfectly good job for you and enjoy themselves at the same time.

Opening Hours

To complete your makeover, you may need to expand your opening hours. Most shops these days are open at least sixty hours a week, and open seven days a week. They have learned to do this without increasing their costs, because for most of them, the net effect has not brought an increase in income. Libraries have to learn to do the same.

Each situation is different, but the starting point is to identify any staff who would prefer to work different hours, thus providing opportunities to stay open longer. Councils sometimes have strange employment practices, which often are not part of contracts or legal agreements but have become traditional. Quite often, a free and open discussion among staff will reveal many possibilities for extending hours.

Role of Librarian and the Staff

Whatever you have planned for the stock, the building, and the opening hours, the community's response to and sense of the place comes from the people who work in the library.

Librarians know there is no greater satisfaction than being able to assist a customer: discovering a book that a small child enjoys reading, helping a person trace a relative, obtaining a hard-to-find book from an overseas academic database for a patron, guiding a novice through the World Wide Web, or just recommending a good book to read. Enjoy the accomplishment and be proud. You do an incredibly important job.

Behind the Scenes

The points so far have been about customer experience and the staff's role in providing it. Retailers concentrate on these matters, because if their competitors are better they will lose their income. But they have to make sure that as much as possible of their income is devoted to the customer experience and as little as possible is taken up behind the scenes, or in overhead or management costs of any kind. The makeover of a library is an opportunity to address many of the areas of behind-the-scenes costs and, as far as possible, to eliminate them.

The reading of all good books is like conversation
with the finest men of past centuries.

—DESCARTES

Too much precious library money is spent on employees working at computer screens on repetitive and often meaningless paperwork, or closing libraries, and packing and unpacking books, and not much is spent on the library. We move books too often at great cost to both our budget and our environment. We have to tackle these problems, even though it will be difficult to do so.

In England, national initiatives are intended to help councils reduce some of these costs, but the truth is that whatever the outcome of these reviews, it still falls to councils, and to individual libraries, to effect the actual cost savings. It is not enough to sit back and wait for the result of the reports. There is plenty of savings work that can begin now.

There is no need, for example, for an individual library to conduct much of the following behind-the-scenes work. Costs such as these could be examined carefully during a makeover:

- Bibliographic service, cataloguing, and labelling are no longer necessary with "shelf-ready stock."
- Library-maintained catalogues can be replaced by better supplier-provided catalogues which are designed to be reader friendly, eliminating costs to the council.
- Bid documents and contracts can be greatly simplified and their preparation time reduced substantially.
- Much of the time spent on stock selection can be reduced by using supplier preorders to aid and facilitate the process.
- Electronic data interchange makes reduced invoice handling costs and considerable savings possible.
- Discussions with suppliers (and potential suppliers) at the time of planning the makeover can help identify possible and realistic timescales for achieving these savings.

Launch

When people come to see your new building—aside from the opening day when all the local officials turn up—they will be most interested in the stock. They will come looking for the books on their favourite topics, and this is the moment to make a real impression. You will win them for life if they find something very special and interesting in your new collection. So the end of the refit is not the day the builder leaves or the dignitaries make speeches, but the day the stock is on the shelves, clearly displayed in all its new abundance. This is the day you say, "We are a new library."

After the reopening, go back to your groups of readers, friends, and nonusers, and get them to talk about whether you have corrected any problems or incorporated their requested improvements. You are at the beginning of a new dialogue with your community; regard it as a start, not a finish.

A Charter for Public Libraries

This English village library was dirty and poorly maintained before its makeover. Now, by being open six days a week including during lunchtime, people don't have to try to remember which day it is before they visit. It is very unusual to see English libraries open this much, although, of course, every shop in the same village is open every day, all day.

Some librarians came to believe that they were offering too much choice and that the sizes of the collections were frightening, particularly for teenagers. But at the same time, big bookstore chains were succeeding in attracting adults and teenagers with their huge selections.

The essential value of public libraries needs to be reinforced at both local and national levels. A focused effort by citizens and their local governments, as outlined in the conditions below, will see libraries maintain their role and relevance for generations to come.

1. **Make the libraries local**
   Individual libraries, large and small, need to be empowered and resourced to meet the specific needs of their local communities. The individuality of each library cannot be overstated, and libraries need the freedom to operate independently.

2. **Increase opening hours**
   In today's society it is unforgivable that some libraries close for lunch or on certain weekdays. Providing access to library services means opening libraries at times when the community wants them open; late closing and weekend opening should be the norm.

3. **Improve library collections**
   Library collections—not only books but all other resources—need to be maintained, improved, and accessible. This means increased funding for new stock, replacement stock, and public access to special collections.

4. **Improve the library environment**
   All public libraries should be attractive and dignified places to visit and in which to read and study. They need to be kept clean, safe, and smart. Standards of interior design need to be raised and building architecture used to best effect.

5. **Embrace technology**
   While books should remain the focus for libraries, computers and technology can enhance users' experiences. With this in mind, computers and all associated equipment need to be in good working order and kept up to date.

6. **Liberate librarians**
   The distinction and allocation of roles between "professional" (i.e., "charter qualified") and "nonprofessional" should cease: training is essential for the teams in libraries, whether they are long or short term, full-time or part-time. Volunteers are welcome for many aspects of the service, but they cannot take the place of professional staff in providing day-to-day service to readers.

Classical architecture meets modern needs at the Howell Carnegie District Library in Howell, Michigan. Historical features are preserved (above) and the children's room (below) has updated features tailored to the community's requirements.

7. **Share best practice**
Collaboration between neighbouring authorities will make limited resources go further, and sharing best practice will mean all libraries are better able to meet users' expectations.

8. **Share financial information**
Accurate, meaningful, and consistent reporting of library budgets and expenditure will encourage accountability and openness and mean all budget discussions are grounded in facts.

9. **Provide performance feedback**
Performance reporting should be timely, accurate, and clear. Every month councils should report publicly the key usage figures for each library that they are responsible for.

10. **Engage all stakeholders**
There needs to be substantial genuine effort to build trust between councils, government bodies, library professionals, and library patrons. Local officials must all be fully and properly informed about library matters, and libraries should actively work with patrons and supporters in the community.

11. **Keep libraries alive, even in times of change**
Of course, sometimes building development means that libraries have to move. Residents, however, are often distrustful about these changes. People come to depend on their libraries, and any savings from a library closure will be tiny compared to the animosity generated among library users and citizens at large. In addition, many library patrons belong to groups marginalized by society—the elderly, the unemployed, single-parent families—and the negative impact on these people's lives following library closures will outweigh any cost savings.

12. **Hold officials accountable**
Public-library users should call upon their local officials, whether a London borough council or a Massachusetts selectboard, to commit themselves to achieving the aims of this charter.

A Message to Government

The public library service needs a clear and straightforward vision statement that the service is for books, reading, and information, and that it provides a private place for reading and study. Libraries and the library service should be of the highest quality, accessible to all, and inviting to use.

In the United Kingdom the public library service is operated and funded by local councils, but the overall responsibility for the service in the end lies with the national government. They both need to have a clearer understanding of their roles and responsibilities. The government should understand that the service belongs to the public, and they should accept responsibility for the service's operation. They should acknowledge their duty to pass on the service, buildings, and collections to future generations.

Councils should publicly acknowledge and clearly state that they share this same vision of the library service with the government. It is not for individual councils to redefine what the public library service means, but rather to operate and provide the service to the public.

The service's performance and costs should be measured independently of national and local government by one or more consumer associations who are tasked to gather and report information on behalf of the public. This information should be available and communicated to the public and councils.

New, independently provided training programmes (funded by councils) which use the performance and cost data supplied by these new agencies should be prepared for councillors who are responsible for libraries, directors of councils, library managers, and council officers who operate the public library service. The whole training and management development regime for public libraries needs renewal. The traditional demarcation between "professional" and "nonprofessional" staff should be stopped. All staff, long or short term, full- or part-time, should be properly trained to give a high and professional standard of service.

Councils need to devolve library management to local libraries and find practical ways to build relationships with and involve the public in the community that surrounds each library. They should, in doing so, reduce the level of nonlibrary operations and seek to outsource administrative work.

There needs to be a substantial effort to rebuild the trust between library users and those who operate the service. For too long, the agendas for change have been unresponsive to readers and disconnected from the public need. That situation must be put right. The public library service should not be measured by its contribution to other government agendas, but against its own values, which are extraordinary and sufficient.

Major Organizations and Resources

American Library Association (ALA)
www.ala.org

Booklist Magazine
www.booklistonline.com

The Bookseller
www.thebookseller.com

The Campaign for the Book
http://alangibbons.net

Chartered Institute of Library and Information Professionals (CILIP)
www.cilip.org.uk

Department for Culture, Media and Sport (DCMS)
www.culture.gov.uk

European Bureau of Library, Information and Documentation Associations (EBLIDA)
www.eblida.org

The International Federation of Library Associations and Institutions (IFLA)
www.ifla.org

Libraries for Life for Londoners (LLL)
www.librarylondon.org

The Library Campaign
www.librarycampaign.com/Home

Library Journal
www.libraryjournal.com

Library Web (UK)
www.libraryweb.info

Museums, Libraries and Archives Council (MLA)
www.mla.gov.uk

Publishers Weekly
www.publishersweekly.com

The Reading Agency (TRA)
www.readingagency.org.uk

Save Old Town Library
http://friendsofoldtownlibrary.co.uk/SaveOTLibraryHome.htm

Society of Chief Librarians (SCL)
www.goscl.com

About the Author

Library campaigner Tim Coates is, according to the website TheBookseller.com, "an outspoken champion of the absolutely central place of books in libraries." Surprising as it may sound, his conviction that libraries are first and foremost a place for books and reading has brought him into conflict in England with the government ministers responsible for libraries and with professional library associations. His Good Library Guide Blog is said to be read at 10 Downing Street, especially during times when library closures attract national press coverage, and the British Library has archived the blog as part of its work to ensure the preservation of the United Kingdom's historical documents.

It is not so surprising that Coates is a passionate proponent of books, given that earlier in his thirty-five-year career he doubled book sales while reorganizing and redesigning the stores of WH Smith, a leading U.K. bookseller. His efforts earned him praise from the British publisher and philanthropist Paul Hamlyn, who called him "the best bookseller in England." After serving as managing director at Waterstone's, the largest U.K. specialist bookseller, he applied his book trade experience to public libraries. He gave advice to a number of national and government bodies and local councils, and then notably was invited to give his attention to the libraries of the London borough of Hillingdon. In this makeover project (the results of which feature largely throughout this book), Tim worked closely with the council. As a result of it, use of the libraries and book lending have more than doubled, while at the same time budgets have been substantially reduced.

In 2010, he was elected chair of Libraries for Life for Londoners, which campaigns for more support for London's nearly four hundred public libraries.

Coates grew up in the north of England and was educated at Oxford University. His addiction to reading includes studies of nineteenth-century government papers and novels, several of which he has republished. He has written a number of books, the latest of which is *Delane's War*, about the nineteenth-century *London Times* editor John Delane and the Crimean War.

Credits and Information

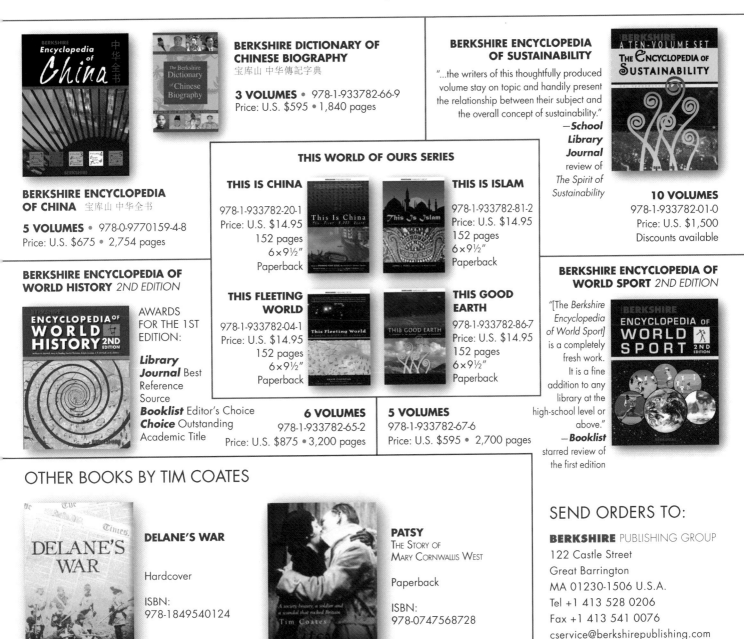

CPSIA information can be obtained at www.ICGtesting.com
Printed in the USA
LVIW01n1710070815
449276LV00008B/69